# Southern Living

# best loved cookies

## 50 *melt in your mouth Southern morsels*

# Southern Living

## best loved cookies

50 melt in your mouth Southern morsels

©2008 by Oxmoor House, Inc.
Book Division of Southern Progress Corporation
P. O. Box 2262, Birmingham, Alabama 35201-2262

*Southern Living*® is a federally registered trademark belonging to Southern Living, Inc.

ISBN-13: 978-0-8487-3262-2
ISBN-10: 0-8487-3262-6
Library of Congress Control Number: 2007942463
Printed in the United States of America
Second Printing 2009

Oxmoor House, Inc.
Editor in Chief: Nancy Fitzpatrick Wyatt
Executive Editor: Susan Carlisle Payne
Art Director: Keith McPherson
Managing Editor: Allison Long Lowery

**Southern Living**® **Best Loved Cookies**
Editor: Susan Hernandez Ray
Project Editor: Julie Boston
Senior Designer: Melissa Jones Clark
Copy Chief: L. Amanda Owens
Editorial Assistant: Vanessa Rusch Thomas
Director, Test Kitchens: Elizabeth Tyler Austin
Assistant Director, Test Kitchens: Julie Christopher
Test Kitchens Professionals: Jane Chambliss; Patricia Michaud; Kathleen Royal Phillips;
    Catherine Crowell Steele; Ashley T. Strickland; Kate Wheeler, R.D.
Photography Director: Jim Bathie
Photographers: Ralph Anderson, Mary M. Chambliss, Van Chaplin, Gary Clark,
    Joe Descoise, William Dickey, Beth Dreiling, Meg McKinney, Art Meripol
Senior Photo Stylist: Kay E. Clarke
Associate Photo Stylist: Katherine G. Eckert
Director of Production: Laura Lockhart
Production Manager: Tamara B. Nall

**Contributors**
Writer: Deborah Garrison Lowery
Compositor: Carol O. Loria
Editorial Contributor: Rebecca R. Benton
Proofreader: Adrienne S. Davis
Indexer: Mary Ann Laurens
Editorial Assistant: Kevin Pearsall
Editorial Interns: Erin Loudy, Anne-Harris Jones, Shea Staskowki, Lauren Wiygul
Photographer: Lee Harrelson
Photo Stylists: Melanie J. Clarke, Katie Stoddard

To order additional publications, call 1-800-765-6400.
For more books to enrich your life, visit **oxmoorhouse.com**
To search, savor, and share thousands of recipes, visit **myrecipes.com**

Cover: Peanut Butter-Toffee Turtle Cookies (page 29),
    Double Chocolate Chunk-Peanut Cookies (page 38),
    Thumbprint Cookies (page 46), Chocolate-Orange Swirls (page 65),
    Molasses-Spice Crinkles (page 42), Classic Sugar Cookies (page 62)

# contents

# my cookie confessions

One of my favorite times with my two daughters is when we make cookies for Santa on Christmas Eve. I started the tradition when Tallulah, my oldest, was 3. I still love looking at the pictures of her in her child-size apron decorated with animals, wielding a small rolling pin. I'm not sure which of us had more fun that afternoon.

It's appropriate that our first food bonding experience was over cookies. I've never been a huge dessert lover, but let a plate of peanut butter or sugar cookies cross my path, and I'm likely to devour the entire thing. So the girls and I always make sure that we store Santa's portion of the batch in a safe place before Dad starts munching.

Assuming that you, too, like cookies (and who doesn't?), we believe you'll love this book. We asked our staff for their favorites and scoured our archives to find the very best recipes. We selected them on flavor, texture, appearance, and ease of preparation.

You won't want to miss specialty cookies, such as Mississippi Mud, Crispy Praline, and tangy Key Lime Squares with Macadamia Crust. Standards get star treatment here, as in Ultimate Chocolate Chip Cookies, White Chocolate Chip-Oatmeal Cookies, and super-rich Peanut Butter-Toffee Turtle Cookies. In short, these are the finest cookies that Southern bakers have to offer. All are so delicious that you may as well make a double batch—you're going to need them.

One word of caution—once you try these home-baked gems, your family will never be satisfied with cookies from refrigerated dough again. So pull out the mixer, turn on the oven, and start baking memories.

Happy cooking!

Scott Jones
Executive Editor, *Southern Living* magazine

# top 10 cookie tips

- **Butter basics.** Avoid using tub butter or margarine products labeled spread, reduced-calorie, liquid, or soft-style; they contain less fat than regular butter or margarine and do not make satisfactory substitutions.
- **Mixing.** Stir or mix dough just until the flour disappears. Overmixing toughens the dough. Prevent stiff cookie dough from straining handheld portable mixers by stirring in the last additions of flour by hand.
- **Greasing pans.** Lightly grease baking sheets only if the recipe specifies it, and use only vegetable cooking spray or solid shortening, not butter or margarine.
- **Baking sheets.** Use shiny, heavy, aluminum baking sheets. Dark sheets may absorb heat, causing cookies to brown too much on the bottom; nonstick baking sheets work well if they are not too dark. Insulated baking sheets require a slightly longer baking time.
- **Oven rack.** Bake one batch at a time on the middle rack; if you have to bake two at a time, rotate them from top to bottom halfway through baking.
- **Always preheat the oven and bake with precision.** If you prefer soft and chewy cookies, take them out of the oven at the lower end of time. If you prefer crisper cookies, leave them in one or two minutes longer.

- **Cooling.** Unless the recipe states otherwise, remove cookies from baking sheets immediately after removal from oven. Transfer cookies to a wire rack to cool, being careful not to stack them or to let the sides touch. Cookies firm up as they cool.
- **Time-saving tip.** When baking many batches of cookies, spoon the dough onto sheets of parchment paper, assembly-line fashion. Then slide each batch onto a baking sheet when ready to bake. Using parchment paper eliminates the need to grease the baking sheets.
- **Storing.** Store soft, chewy cookies in an airtight container and crisp cookies in a container with a loose-fitting lid. Store bar cookies in their baking pan; seal the top of the pan with aluminum foil. Unfrosted bar cookies can be stacked and stored in airtight containers.
- **Freezing.** Unfrosted cookies freeze well for eight months in zip-top plastic freezer bags, metal tins, or plastic freezer containers. Dough can be frozen up to six months. Thaw dough in the refrigerator or at room temperature until it's the right consistency for shaping.

**Chunky Chocolate Gobs,** page 17

# drop cookies

These are the kinds of cookies you make when you're in a hurry. No flour-covered counters or sticky rolling pins. Even 2-year-olds can drop the dough from a spoon, so the experience is all fun and no fuss…for everyone.

**Here are a few of our favorite tips:**

• We used teaspoons (not measuring spoons) for scooping and dropping dough. Simply scoop up the desired amount of dough with one spoon, and use the back of another to push the dough onto the baking sheet.

• You can also use a cookie scoop, which looks like a small ice-cream scoop, to drop the dough onto the baking sheet. These scoops come in a variety of sizes, from 1 teaspoon to several tablespoons.

• Whatever you decide to use to scoop out the dough, coat it with cooking spray first to encourage easy release.

• Take care to scoop equal amounts of dough each time so cookies will be about the same size. Allow 1 to 2 inches between balls of dough on the baking sheet so they won't run together as they bake.

• Don't worry about flattening the scooped dough; it will spread and flatten as it bakes.

# white chocolate chip-oatmeal cookies

Keep the ingredients for these quick favorites on hand for an anytime treat.

prep: 15 min.    cook: 12 min. per batch    makes about 5 dozen

1    cup butter or margarine, softened
1    cup firmly packed light brown sugar
1    cup granulated sugar
2    large eggs
2    tsp. vanilla extract
3    cups all-purpose flour
1    tsp. baking soda
1    tsp. baking powder
1    tsp. salt
1½   cups uncooked regular oats
2    cups white chocolate morsels
1    cup coarsely chopped pecans

**1.** Beat butter at medium speed with an electric mixer until creamy; gradually add sugars, beating well. Add eggs, 1 at a time, beating just until yellow disappears after each addition. Stir in vanilla.

**2.** Combine flour and next 3 ingredients; gradually add to butter mixture, beating until blended. Stir in oats, morsels, and pecans.

**3.** Drop dough by tablespoonfuls onto greased baking sheets.

**4.** Bake at 350° for 12 minutes. Cool on baking sheets 3 minutes; remove to wire racks to cool completely.

# ultimate chocolate chip cookies

Dark brown sugar adds surprising richness to this cookie dough. Bake each batch 8 minutes for soft and gooey cookies, or up to 14 minutes for crisp results.

prep: 30 min.　cook: 14 min. per batch　makes 5 dozen

¾ cup butter, softened

¾ cup granulated sugar

¾ cup firmly packed dark brown sugar

2 large eggs

1½ tsp. vanilla extract

2¼ cups plus 2 Tbsp. all-purpose flour

1 tsp. baking soda

¾ tsp. salt

1 (12-oz.) package semisweet chocolate morsels

**1.** Beat butter and sugars at medium speed with an electric mixer until creamy. Add eggs and vanilla, beating until blended.

**2.** Combine flour, baking soda, and salt in a small bowl; gradually add to butter mixture, beating well. Stir in morsels.

**3.** Drop dough by tablespoonfuls onto ungreased baking sheets.

**4.** Bake at 350° for 8 to 14 minutes or until desired degree of doneness. Remove to wire racks to cool completely.

## variations:

**Peanut Butter-Chocolate Chip Cookies:** Decrease salt to ½ tsp. Add 1 cup creamy peanut butter with butter and sugars. Increase flour to 2½ cups plus 2 Tbsp. Proceed as directed. (Dough will look a little moist.)

**Pecan-Chocolate Chip Cookies:** Add 1½ cups chopped, toasted pecans with chocolate morsels. Proceed as directed.

**Almond-Toffee Chocolate Chip Cookies:** Reduce chocolate morsels to 1 cup. Add ½ cup slivered, toasted almonds and 1 cup toffee bits (we tested with Hershey's Heath Bits O' Brickle Toffee Bits). Proceed as directed.

# chocolate chunk cookies with mocha frosting

prep: 25 min.   cook: 12 min. per batch   other: 32 min.   **makes 3 dozen**

2¼ cups all-purpose flour

⅔ cup unsweetened cocoa

1 tsp. baking soda

¼ tsp. salt

1 cup butter, softened

¾ cup granulated sugar

⅔ cup firmly packed brown sugar

1 tsp. vanilla extract

2 large eggs

1 (11.5-oz.) package semisweet chocolate chunks

Mocha Frosting

**1.** Combine first 4 ingredients in a bowl.

**2.** Beat butter and next 3 ingredients at medium speed with an electric mixer until creamy. Add eggs, 1 at a time, beating just until blended after each addition. Gradually add flour mixture, beating at low speed until blended. Stir in chocolate chunks.

**3.** Drop dough by heaping tablespoonfuls onto parchment paper-lined baking sheets.

**4.** Bake at 350° for 10 to 12 minutes or until puffy. Cool on baking sheets 2 minutes; remove to wire racks, and let cool 30 minutes or until completely cool. Spread cookies with Mocha Frosting.

**Note:** Dough may be refrigerated up to 2 days or frozen up to 1 month. Let come to room temperature before baking as directed.

## mocha frosting

prep: 10 min.   makes about 3 cups

½ cup butter, softened

4 cups powdered sugar

2 to 3 Tbsp. half-and-half

3 Tbsp. strong brewed coffee (cooled)

**1.** Beat butter at medium speed with an electric mixer until creamy; gradually add powdered sugar and remaining ingredients, beating until smooth.

# chunky chocolate gobs

These ultrachocolate cookies are, hands down, some of the best ever to come through our Test Kitchens.

prep: 18 min.   cook: 12 min. per batch   other: 40 min.   makes about 2½ dozen

¾ cup unsalted butter, softened

⅓ cup butter-flavored shortening

1 cup granulated sugar

⅔ cup firmly packed dark brown sugar

2 large eggs

2 tsp. vanilla extract

2 cups all-purpose flour

⅔ cup unsweetened cocoa

1 tsp. baking soda

¼ tsp. salt

2 cups cream-filled chocolate sandwich cookies, coarsely chopped (16 cookies)

3 (1.75-oz.) Mounds bars, chilled and chopped

1 to 2 cups semisweet chocolate morsels

**1.** Beat butter and shortening at medium speed with an electric mixer until creamy; gradually add sugars, beating until light and fluffy. Add eggs and vanilla, beating until blended.

**2.** Combine flour and next 3 ingredients; gradually add to butter mixture, beating until blended. Stir in cookies, candy bars, and desired amount of chocolate morsels. Chill dough 30 minutes.

**3.** Drop dough by ¼ cupfuls 2 inches apart onto parchment paper-lined baking sheets.

**4.** Bake at 350° for 10 to 12 minutes or until barely set. Cool on baking sheets 10 minutes. Remove to wire racks to cool completely.

*Delights from the Delta* Just like the banks of the Mississippi River, these cookies are ooey, gooey, and chocolate brown. The original Mississippi mud cake is thought to have been created by World War II-era cooks who found a way to use available ingredients to make a dense chocolate cake. Marshmallows pressed into the dough make these cookies just as dense and sweet as the famous cake. And like the cake, they go best with a huge scoop of vanilla ice cream.

## Mississippi mud cookies

**prep: 25 min.   cook: 12 min. per batch**   makes about 3 dozen

1   cup semisweet chocolate morsels
½   cup butter, softened
1   cup sugar
2   large eggs
1   tsp. vanilla extract
1½  cups all-purpose flour
1   tsp. baking powder
½   tsp. salt
1   cup chopped pecans
½   cup milk chocolate morsels
1   cup plus 2 Tbsp. miniature marshmallows

**1.** Microwave semisweet chocolate morsels in a small microwave-safe glass bowl at HIGH 1 minute or until smooth, stirring every 30 seconds.

**2.** Beat butter and sugar at medium speed with an electric mixer until creamy; add eggs, 1 at a time, beating until blended after each addition. Beat in vanilla and melted chocolate.

**3.** Combine flour, baking powder, and salt; gradually add to chocolate mixture, beating until well blended. Stir in chopped pecans and ½ cup milk chocolate morsels.

**4.** Drop dough by heaping tablespoonfuls onto parchment paper-lined baking sheets. Press 3 marshmallows into each portion of dough.

**5.** Bake at 350° for 10 to 12 minutes or until set. Remove to wire racks to cool completely.

# brownie cookies

You'll love how these scrumptious double-chocolate cookies are similar in texture to thick and fudgy brownies.

prep: 15 min.    cook: 10 min. per batch    makes 2½ dozen

½   cup butter

4   (1-oz.) unsweetened chocolate baking
    squares, chopped

3   cups semisweet chocolate morsels,
    divided

1½  cups all-purpose flour

½   tsp. baking powder

½   tsp. salt

4   large eggs

1½  cups sugar

2   tsp. vanilla extract

2   cups chopped pecans, toasted

**1.** Combine butter, unsweetened chocolate, and 1½ cups chocolate morsels in a large heavy saucepan. Cook over low heat, stirring constantly, until butter and chocolate melt; cool.

**2.** Combine flour, baking powder, and salt; set aside.

**3.** Beat eggs, sugar, and vanilla at medium speed with an electric mixer. Gradually add flour mixture to egg mixture, beating well. Add chocolate mixture; beat well. Stir in remaining 1½ cups chocolate morsels and pecans.

**4.** Drop dough by 2 tablespoonfuls 1 inch apart onto parchment paper-lined baking sheets.

**5.** Bake at 350° for 10 minutes. Cool slightly on baking sheets; remove to wire racks to cool completely.

*Let it snow!* Most Southerners get excited about a few flakes in the sky, but the highest elevations of the Smoky Mountains of Tennessee and North Carolina get an average snowfall of 69 inches each winter. Reminiscent of the white-dusted mountain peaks, these cookies, with white chocolate and a dusting of powdered sugar, are as sweet as snowfall on a school day in the South. Toasted walnuts and nutmeg give them a nice crunch and spicy flavor.

## Smoky Mountain snowcaps

prep: 25 min.   cook: 12 min. per batch   **makes 3½ dozen**

6   oz. white chocolate, chopped
¾   cup butter or margarine, softened
1   cup sugar
3   large eggs
1   tsp. vanilla extract
3½  cups all-purpose flour
1   tsp. baking powder
¾   tsp. salt
⅛   tsp. ground nutmeg
1½  cups chopped walnuts, toasted
½   cup powdered sugar

**1.** Melt white chocolate in a small saucepan over low heat, stirring until chocolate is smooth.

**2.** Beat butter and 1 cup sugar at medium speed with an electric mixer 5 minutes or until fluffy. Add eggs, 1 at a time, beating until blended after each addition. Add vanilla, beating well. Add melted chocolate, and beat 30 seconds.

**3.** Combine flour and next 3 ingredients; add to butter mixture, beating until blended. Stir in walnuts.

**4.** Drop dough by heaping tablespoonfuls onto lightly greased baking sheets.

**5.** Bake at 350° for 10 to 12 minutes or until edges are lightly browned. Remove to wire racks to cool completely. Sprinkle with powdered sugar. Freeze up to 1 month in an airtight container, if desired.

# toffee-oatmeal cookies

Buttery toffee adds a delicious flavor to these chewy oatmeal cookies.

**prep: 15 min.    cook: 10 min. per batch    makes 4 dozen**

½    cup butter or margarine, softened
½    cup firmly packed brown sugar
2    large eggs
1    tsp. vanilla extract
1½   cups uncooked regular oats
1    cup all-purpose flour
½    tsp. baking soda
¼    tsp. salt
½    cup chopped pecans
1½   cups (8 oz.) toffee bits (we tested with Hershey's
     Heath Bits O' Brickle Toffee Bits)

**1.** Beat butter at medium speed with an electric mixer
2 to 3 minutes or until creamy. Add sugar, beating
well. Add eggs and vanilla, beating until blended.
**2.** Combine oats and next 3 ingredients; add to butter
mixture, beating just until blended. Stir in chopped
pecans and toffee bits.
**3.** Drop dough by heaping tablespoonfuls onto lightly
greased baking sheets.
**4.** Bake at 375° for 10 minutes. Remove to wire racks
to cool completely.

# chocolate-and-almond macaroons

For easy cleanup, place a sheet of wax paper under the wire rack to catch the excess chocolate as you drizzle it on the cookies.

prep: 15 min.   cook: 17 min. per batch   makes 2 dozen

¾   cup sweetened condensed milk
1   (14-oz.) package sweetened flaked coconut
¼   to ½ tsp. almond extract
⅛   tsp. salt
24  whole unblanched almonds
½   cup dark chocolate morsels

**1.** Stir together first 4 ingredients.

**2.** Drop dough by lightly greased tablespoonfuls onto parchment paper-lined baking sheets. Press an almond into the top of each cookie.

**3.** Bake at 350° for 15 to 17 minutes or until golden. Remove to wire racks to cool.

**4.** Microwave ½ cup chocolate morsels in a microwave-safe bowl at HIGH 1 minute and 15 seconds or until melted and smooth, stirring at 30-second intervals and at end. Transfer to a 1-qt. zip-top plastic freezer bag; cut a tiny hole in 1 corner of bag. Pipe melted chocolate over cooled cookies by gently squeezing bag.

# crunchy frostbite cookies

Just a touch of peppermint extract adds the frosty flavor to the icing in this melt-in-your-mouth favorite.

prep: 22 min.    cook: 14 min. per batch    other: 1 hr.    **makes about 3 dozen**

2    cups all-purpose flour
2    tsp. baking soda
1    tsp. baking powder
¼    tsp. salt
1    cup shortening
¾    cup granulated sugar
¾    cup firmly packed light brown sugar
2    large eggs
1    tsp. vanilla extract
1½    cups uncooked regular oats
1½    cups cornflakes cereal
2    (6-oz.) packages white chocolate baking squares, chopped
3    Tbsp. shortening
½    tsp. peppermint extract

**1.** Combine first 4 ingredients; stir well until blended. Beat 1 cup shortening at medium speed with an electric mixer until creamy; gradually add sugars, beating well. Add eggs and vanilla; beat well. Add flour mixture, mixing just until blended. Stir in oats and cornflakes.
**2.** Drop dough by heaping tablespoonfuls, 2 inches apart, onto lightly greased baking sheets; flatten slightly.
**3.** Bake at 325° for 12 to 14 minutes. Cool slightly on baking sheets. Remove to wire racks to cool completely.
**4.** Microwave white chocolate and 3 Tbsp. shortening in a medium-size microwave-safe bowl at HIGH 1 minute or until white chocolate melts, stirring once. Stir in peppermint extract. Dip flat bottom of each cookie into melted white chocolate, letting excess drip back into bowl. Place dipped cookies, dipped side up, on wax paper, and let stand 1 hour or until white chocolate sets.

*Double-nut flavor* Traditional turtle candy calls for chocolate, caramels, and pecan halves to be molded into the shape of a turtle. For these cookies, traditional turtle candy flavors are teamed with creamy peanut butter for a Southern touch.

## peanut butter-toffee turtle cookies

prep: 25 min.   cook: 12 min. per batch   makes 3 dozen

⅔   cup creamy peanut butter
½   cup unsalted butter, softened
½   cup granulated sugar
½   cup firmly packed light brown sugar
1   large egg
2   cups all-purpose baking mix
⅔   cup toffee bits
⅔   cup coarsely chopped peanuts
⅔   cup milk chocolate morsels
10   oz. vanilla caramels
2   to 3 Tbsp. whipping cream
½   tsp. vanilla extract
Pecan halves
⅔   cup milk chocolate morsels

**1.** Beat first 4 ingredients at medium speed with an electric mixer until creamy. Add egg, beating until blended. Add baking mix, beating at low speed just until blended. Stir in toffee bits, chopped peanuts, and ⅔ cup chocolate morsels.

**2.** Drop dough by rounded tablespoonfuls onto ungreased baking sheets; flatten dough with hand.

**3.** Bake at 350° for 10 to 12 minutes or until golden brown. Cool on baking sheets 1 minute; remove to wire racks to cool completely.

**4.** Microwave caramels and 2 Tbsp. cream in a microwave-safe bowl at HIGH 1 minute; stir. Continue to microwave at 30-second intervals, stirring until caramels melt and mixture is smooth; add additional cream, if necessary. Stir in vanilla. Spoon mixture onto tops of cookies; top with pecan halves.

**5.** Microwave ⅔ cup chocolate morsels in a microwave-safe bowl at HIGH 1 minute and 15 seconds or until melted and smooth, stirring at 30-second intervals. Transfer to a 1-qt. zip-top plastic freezer bag; cut a tiny hole in 1 corner of bag. Pipe melted chocolate over cookies by squeezing bag.

*A taste of the Big Easy* In Louisiana it's "prah·leen." In Georgia it's "pray·leen." But no matter where you're from, these cookies remind you of the beloved pecan candy tradition from New Orleans, on the Mississippi River, where sugar cane and nuts were cultivated in abundance. The original version contained almonds. Those were replaced with Louisiana pecans, and a Southern specialty was born. Throughout the French Quarter, shops entice passersby with the rich confection of caramelized sugar, pecans, butter, and vanilla.

## crispy praline cookies

**prep: 10 min.   cook: 15 min. per batch**   makes 2 dozen

½   cup butter, softened
1   cup firmly packed dark brown sugar
1   large egg
1   tsp. vanilla extract
1   cup all-purpose flour
1   cup chopped pecans

**1.** Beat butter and sugar at medium speed with an electric mixer until creamy; add egg beating just until blended. Add vanilla, and mix well.
**2.** Gradually add flour, beating just until blended. Stir in pecans.
**3.** Drop dough by tablespoonfuls onto parchment paper-lined baking sheets.
**4.** Bake at 350° for 13 to 15 minutes. Cool on baking sheets 1 minute, then remove to racks to cool completely.

## variation:

**Crispy Praline-Chocolate Chip Cookies:** Add 1 cup semisweet chocolate morsels, and bake as directed.

Cocoa-Almond Biscotti, page 53

# shaped
# cookies

Rolled into balls or logs, fashioned into crescents, or indented to hold a little lake of jelly or frosting, dough for shaped cookies is fun to work with. Sometimes the dough needs to chill to make it easy to shape, but it's definitely worth the wait. The unique shapes make these cookies look extra special for teas, dessert buffets, cookie swaps, gifts, or just plain indulging.

## Here are hints for this type of cookie:

- If dough seems too soft to shape, chill it for an hour or so until it's firm enough.
- Coat hands with cooking spray before handling the dough to prevent it from sticking.
- If shaping dough into balls, roll it with the palms of your hands.
- When shaping balls of dough, roll all balls the same size so cookies will be uniform after baking.
- Use a ruler or measuring spoon for the first few cookies to help you determine the right size; then you can judge the rest by eye.

- If your recipe calls for flattening the dough balls, use the bottom of a glass. Coat the bottom of the glass with cooking spray after every three or four cookies.
- Slice-and-bake cookies are notable for their make-ahead quality. You can roll the dough into a log, chill it up to a week or freeze it up to a month. When it's baking time, just slice the dough directly from the refrigerator or freezer, and bake only the number of cookies you want. If you don't bake all the cookies at once, return the remaining dough to the refrigerator or freezer to use later.

*Cookies from the garden* Go to your herb garden to turn this simple cookie recipe into something fancy. In Colonial days, when spices were hard to come by, Southern cooks made much use of fresh herbs, even for desserts such as pound cakes, sorbets, and cookies. These sugar-sprinkled cookies with a trace of lemony-flavored basil are perfect for tea parties and special holiday gifts. Garnish a platter of them with fresh basil sprigs, unless you'd like to keep your guests guessing about the "secret" ingredient.

# lemon-basil butter cookies

**prep: 20 min.     cook: 10 min. per batch     makes 6½ dozen**

1     cup fresh lemon-basil leaves*
1¾   cups sugar, divided
1     lb. butter, softened
¼    cup lemon juice
1     large egg
6     cups all-purpose flour
Garnishes: fresh lemon-basil sprigs, lemon wedges

**1.** Process basil and ¼ cup sugar in a food processor until blended.
**2.** Beat butter at medium speed with an electric mixer until creamy; gradually add remaining 1½ cups sugar, beating well. Add lemon juice and egg, beating until blended. Gradually add flour and basil mixture, beating until blended.
**3.** Shape dough into 1-inch balls, and place 2 inches apart on lightly greased baking sheets. Flatten slightly with bottom of a glass dipped in sugar.
**4.** Bake at 350° for 8 to 10 minutes or until lightly browned. Remove to wire racks to cool completely. Garnish, if desired.

*Plain fresh basil leaves may be substituted for lemon-basil leaves.

# chocolate-espresso shortbread

Edges tipped with unsweetened chocolate and white chocolate enhance the coffee flavor in these elegant cookies.

**prep: 33 min.   cook: 23 min.   makes 1½ to 2 dozen**

1¼   cups all-purpose flour

¼   cup cornstarch

¼   cup unsweetened cocoa

1   tsp. instant espresso powder or instant coffee powder (we tested with Café Bustelo)

¼   tsp. salt

1   cup unsalted butter, softened

1   cup powdered sugar

3   (1-oz.) unsweetened chocolate baking squares

3   oz. white chocolate baking bar (we tested with Ghirardelli)

**1.** Combine first 5 ingredients in a medium bowl; set aside.

**2.** Beat butter at medium speed with an electric mixer until creamy; gradually add powdered sugar, beating well. Stir in dry ingredients; beat just until blended.

**3.** Line 2 baking sheets with parchment paper. Divide dough into 3 equal portions. Place 2 dough portions on opposite ends of 1 baking sheet. Place remaining portion on second baking sheet.

**4.** Cover dough portions with plastic wrap; gently press or roll each portion into a 5½-inch circle. Lightly score each round with a sharp knife into 6 or 8 wedges.

**5.** Bake rounds at 325° for 23 minutes or until shortbread feels firm to the touch. Gently score each round again with a sharp knife. Slide parchment from baking sheets onto wire racks. Let shortbread cool completely on parchment. Cut shortbread into wedges along scored lines.

**6.** Melt chocolate baking bars separately in small bowls in the microwave according to package directions. Partially dip one corner of the wide end of each shortbread wedge in unsweetened chocolate. Place on a wax paper-lined jelly-roll pan, and freeze briefly to set chocolate. Then partially dip other corner of wide end of each wedge in white chocolate. Freeze briefly to set white chocolate.

*Peanut power!* Even before Jimmy Carter brought attention to the goodness of goobers grown in Georgia and Alabama, Southerners found innumerable ways to enjoy their peanuts: in peanut butter—creamy or chunky; dry-roasted; salted; boiled; and honeyed. Chunky peanut butter and dry-roasted peanuts make these chocolate cookies irresistible. A dash of cinnamon gives them an unexpected flavor. They are easy to make, and the balls of dough bake into nice round shapes just perfect for your next cookie swap.

## double chocolate chunk-peanut cookies

prep: 20 min.  cook: 15 min. per batch  **makes 28 cookies**

½   cup butter, softened
½   cup shortening
1   cup chunky peanut butter
1   cup granulated sugar
1   cup firmly packed brown sugar
2   large eggs
2   cups all-purpose flour
⅓   cup unsweetened cocoa, sifted
1½ tsp. baking soda
1   tsp. baking powder
½   tsp. salt
1   tsp. ground cinnamon
1   cup unsalted dry-roasted peanuts
1   (11.5-oz.) package chocolate chunks

**1.** Beat butter and shortening at medium speed with an electric mixer until creamy; add chunky peanut butter and sugars, beating well. Add eggs, beating until blended.

**2.** Combine flour and next 5 ingredients. Add to butter mixture, beating well.

**3.** Stir in peanuts and chocolate chunks.

**4.** Shape dough into 2-inch balls (about 2 Tbsp. for each cookie). Place 2 inches apart on ungreased baking sheets, and flatten cookies slightly.

**5.** Bake at 375° for 12 to 15 minutes or until lightly browned. Cool cookies on baking sheets for 1 to 2 minutes, and remove cookies to wire racks to cool completely.

# chocolate wedding cookies

Powdered sugar blended with cocoa dusts these cookies for a novel flavor twist to an old favorite. Serve these treats for any special occasion.

**prep: 23 min.    cook: 10 min. per batch    makes 2 dozen**

½  cup powdered sugar
2  Tbsp. unsweetened cocoa
½  cup butter or margarine, softened
¾  cup all-purpose flour
⅓  cup granulated sugar
¼  cup unsweetened cocoa
1  tsp. vanilla extract
1  cup finely chopped pecans, toasted

**1.** Sift together powdered sugar and 2 Tbsp. cocoa. Set aside.

**2.** Beat butter at medium speed with an electric mixer until creamy. Add flour and next 3 ingredients, beating until blended. Stir in pecans. (Dough will be stiff.)

**3.** Shape into 1-inch balls, and place on ungreased baking sheets.

**4.** Bake at 400° for 10 minutes. Remove to wire racks, and cool slightly. Roll warm cookies in powdered sugar mixture, and cool completely on wire racks.

*From the good ole days* Remember elementary school, when homemade peanut butter cookies with the classic fork design on top were a lunchroom treat? With only four ingredients in this recipe, you can relive your childhood days in a matter of minutes. Serve them warm from the oven with a tall glass of cold milk.

## easiest peanut butter cookies

prep: 20 min.    cook: 15 min. per batch    **makes 2½ dozen**

1    cup peanut butter
1    cup sugar
1    large egg
1    tsp. vanilla extract

**1.** Combine all ingredients in a large bowl; stir until blended. Shape dough into 1-inch balls. Place balls 1 inch apart on ungreased baking sheets, and flatten gently with tines of a fork.

**2.** Bake at 325° for 15 minutes or until golden brown. Remove to wire racks to cool completely.

*Sweet and spicy* For centuries Southerners have treasured their jars of molasses—the cooked-down sugar cane mixture that is thick, brown, and sticky—with a sharp and tangy flavor. From the hills of Tennessee to the plains of Georgia, the syrup was a table condiment for drizzling on biscuits and pancakes, or stirring into desserts. Still a treat today, the strong, sweet flavor of molasses balances well with a team of spices in these soft, chewy cookies crusted with sugar.

## molasses-spice crinkles

prep: 15 min.   cook: 11 min. per batch   other: 1 hr.   makes 3 dozen

¾  cup shortening
1  cup granulated sugar
1  large egg
¼  cup molasses
2  cups all-purpose flour
1  tsp. baking powder
1  tsp. baking soda
¼  tsp. salt
1  tsp. ground ginger
1  tsp. ground cinnamon
½  tsp. ground nutmeg
¼  tsp. ground cloves
¼  tsp. ground allspice
1  cup sparkling sugar

**1.** Beat shortening at medium speed with an electric mixer until fluffy. Gradually add 1 cup granulated sugar, beating well. Add egg and molasses; beat well.

**2.** Combine flour and next 8 ingredients, stirring well. Add one-fourth of flour mixture at a time to shortening mixture, beating at low speed after each addition until blended. Cover and chill 1 hour.

**3.** Shape dough into 1-inch balls, and roll in sparkling sugar. Place 2 inches apart on ungreased baking sheets.

**4.** Bake at 375° for 9 to 11 minutes. (Tops will crack.) Remove to wire racks to cool completely.

*Who spiked the cookies?* In the early days of the South, the unique corn whiskey made in Kentucky was often referred to as Bourbon, the name of the county in which it was distilled. Today, it means the "good stuff"—or whiskey aged in charred oak barrels for at least two years. Hardly a Christmas can pass in the South without these traditional ball-shaped, bourbon-flavored pecan cookies ending up on a dessert bar or in a gift box.

## bourbon balls

**prep: 28 min.** makes 4 dozen

1   (12-oz.) package vanilla wafers, finely crushed
1   cup chopped pecans or walnuts
¾   cup powdered sugar
2   Tbsp. cocoa
2½  Tbsp. light corn syrup
½   cup bourbon
Powdered sugar

**1.** Combine vanilla wafers, pecans, powdered sugar, and cocoa in a large bowl; stir well.
**2.** Combine corn syrup and bourbon, stirring well. Pour bourbon mixture over wafer mixture; stir until blended. Shape into 1-inch balls; roll in additional powdered sugar. Store in an airtight container up to 2 weeks.

*Bite-size jewels* These cookies have a bit of crunch from the finely chopped pecans, sweetness from the almond extract, and richness from the butter. But it's the thumbprint impressions on top that give them a personal touch. Strawberry and peach jams make beautiful jewel-colored fillings, but you can use other Southern favorite jams, such as blackberry, muscadine, or apple. They're the perfect cookies to make with the kids—let them make the thumbprints and choose the filling.

## thumbprint cookies

prep: 35 min.   cook: 15 min. per batch   other: 1 hr.   makes 3½ dozen

| | |
|---|---|
| 1 | cup butter, softened |
| ¾ | cup sugar |
| 2 | large eggs, separated |
| 1 | tsp. almond extract |
| 2 | cups all-purpose flour |
| ¼ | tsp. salt |
| 1¼ | cups finely chopped pecans |
| ¼ | cup strawberry jam |
| ¼ | cup peach jam |

**1.** Beat butter at medium speed with an electric mixer until creamy; gradually add sugar, beating well. Add egg yolks and almond extract, beating until blended.
**2.** Combine flour and salt; add to butter mixture, beating at low speed until blended. Cover and chill dough 1 hour.
**3.** Shape dough into 1-inch balls. Lightly beat egg whites. Dip each dough ball in egg white; roll in pecans. Place 2 inches apart on ungreased baking sheets. Press thumb in each dough ball to make an indentation.
**4.** Bake at 350° for 15 minutes. Cool 1 minute on baking sheets, and remove to wire racks to cool completely. Press centers again with thumb while cookies are still warm; fill center of each cookie with jam.

# peanut blossom cookies

You'll love these six-ingredient cookies, ready for the oven in 10 minutes.

prep: 10 min.   cook: 10 min. per batch   **makes 4 dozen**

1    (14-oz.) can sweetened condensed milk
¾    cup creamy peanut butter
1    tsp. vanilla extract
2    cups all-purpose baking mix
⅓    cup sugar
1    (9-oz.) package milk chocolate kisses

**1.** Stir together condensed milk, peanut butter, and vanilla, stirring until smooth. Add baking mix, stirring well.

**2.** Shape dough into 1-inch balls; roll in sugar, and place on ungreased baking sheets. Make an indentation in center of each ball with thumb or spoon handle.

**3.** Bake at 375° for 8 to 10 minutes or until lightly browned. Remove cookies from oven, and press a chocolate kiss in center of each cookie. Remove to wire racks to cool completely.

# pecan crescents

These nutty cookies are much like traditional wedding cookies. Let your kids help roll the dough into logs and bend them into shape.

prep: 40 min.    cook: 12 min. per batch    other: 1 hr.    makes about 5 dozen

1    cup pecan halves, toasted
1    cup butter, softened
¾    cup powdered sugar
2    tsp. vanilla extract
2½  cups sifted all-purpose flour
2    cups powdered sugar

**1.** Pulse pecans in a food processor until they are coarse like sand.

**2.** Beat butter and ¾ cup powdered sugar at medium speed with an electric mixer until creamy. Stir in vanilla and ground pecans. Gradually add flour, beating until a soft dough forms. Cover and chill 1 hour.

**3.** Divide dough into 5 portions; divide each portion into 12 pieces. Roll dough pieces into 2-inch logs, curving ends to form crescents. Place on ungreased baking sheets.

**4.** Bake at 350° for 10 to 12 minutes or until lightly browned. Cool on baking sheets 5 minutes. Roll warm cookies in 2 cups powdered sugar. Cool completely on wire racks, and roll cookies in remaining powdered sugar again after cooled.

# cocoa-almond biscotti

Biscotti are elegantly sliced, intensely crunchy Italian cookies, perfect for dunking into a cup of hot coffee. Enjoy them for breakfast or dessert.

**prep: 20 min.** **cook: 41 min.** makes 2 dozen

½ cup butter or margarine, softened
1 cup sugar
2 large eggs
1½ Tbsp. Kahlua or other coffee-flavored liqueur
2½ cups all-purpose flour
1½ tsp. baking powder
¼ tsp. salt
3 Tbsp. Dutch process cocoa or regular unsweetened cocoa
1 (6-oz.) can whole almonds

**1.** Beat butter and sugar in a large bowl at medium speed with an electric mixer until creamy. Add eggs, beating well. Mix in liqueur.

**2.** Combine flour and next 3 ingredients; add to butter mixture, beating at low speed until blended. Stir in almonds.

**3.** Divide dough in half; using floured hands, shape each portion into a 9- x 2-inch log on a lightly greased baking sheet.

**4.** Bake at 350° for 28 to 30 minutes or until firm. Cool on baking sheet 5 minutes. Remove to a wire rack to cool.

**5.** Cut each log diagonally into ¾-inch-thick slices with a serrated knife, using a gentle sawing motion. Place slices on ungreased baking sheets. Bake 5 minutes. Turn cookies over, and bake 5 to 6 more minutes. Remove to wire racks to cool completely.

# biscotti with lavender and orange

Fresh lavender, combined with freshly grated orange rind, gives these crunchy cookies an aromatic appeal that's better than any bakery fare.

prep: 13 min.   cook: 55 min.   makes 15 cookies

½   cup sugar
¼   cup butter, softened
1½ to 2 Tbsp. coarsely chopped fresh lavender
½   tsp. grated orange rind
2   large eggs
2   cups all-purpose flour
2   tsp. baking powder
½   tsp. salt
½   cup sliced almonds, toasted
½   tsp. vanilla extract

**1.** Beat first 4 ingredients at medium speed with an electric mixer until well blended. Add eggs, 1 at a time, beating until blended.

**2.** Combine flour, baking powder, and salt. Gradually add flour mixture to sugar mixture; beat until blended. Stir in almonds and vanilla.

**3.** Using floured hands, shape dough into a 10-inch log on a lightly greased baking sheet, and flatten to 1-inch thickness.

**4.** Bake at 350° for 30 minutes. Remove to a wire rack to cool completely. Reduce oven temperature to 300°.

**5.** Cut log diagonally into ½-inch-thick slices with a serrated knife, using a gentle sawing motion. Place slices on an ungreased baking sheet. Bake at 300° for 20 to 25 minutes (cookies will be slightly soft in center but will harden as they cool). Remove to wire racks to cool completely.

**Date Pinwheel Cookies,** page 73

# rolled & cut cookies

Rolled-and-cut cookies bring Christmas and other special holidays to mind. With these recipes come sprinkles, sparkling sugar, sweet fillings, and decorator icing that make sweet treats come to life. It's a labor of love to create them, but smiling faces make them well worth the effort.

**Keep these tips in mind when rolling dough for cutout or pinwheel cookies:**

- Roll the dough between sheets of heavy-duty plastic wrap to prevent sticking or tearing.
- Place the rolling pin in the center of the dough, and roll outward with soft strokes.
- If the dough becomes soft after rolling, place it in the refrigerator for 10 to 15 minutes or in the freezer for 5 minutes until it firms.
- Dip cookie cutters in flour or powdered sugar to make a clean cutout and to prevent the cutter from sticking to the dough.
- For the cleanest cutouts, when you make an impression with a cookie cutter, cut straight down

into dough—don't twist. Best results come when you're working with a firm or chilled dough that's just been rolled.

- When you begin to cut out cookies, start at the top edge of dough, and make cutouts as close together as possible to get the most yield from the first rolling of the dough. Keep the dough intact until you've cut all the shapes into it; then gather the scraps, knead gently, and reroll. Cut out one more batch of shapes. Do not reroll the scraps again, as the dough will likely be overworked at this point, resulting in cookies that are tough.

# Southern Dutch squares

These cookies are inspired by speculaas, traditional stamped cookies introduced by Dutch settlers who found their way to South Carolina around the 1670s. This variation captures the spiciness and texture of speculaas, but we've skipped the classic wooden stamp, and created simple rolled-and-cut squares pressed with almonds.

**prep: 22 min.   cook: 25 min. per batch**   makes 6 dozen

1    cup butter, softened
¾    cup firmly packed brown sugar
1    large egg
¼    tsp. anise extract or ½ tsp. anise seeds, crushed
⅛    tsp. almond extract
3    cups all-purpose flour
1    Tbsp. baking powder
Pinch of salt
2    tsp. ground cinnamon
¾    tsp. ground cloves
¼    tsp. ground nutmeg
¼    tsp. cocoa
¼    tsp. pepper
½    tsp. grated lemon or orange rind
¼    cup finely chopped blanched almonds
1    (6-oz.) can whole natural almonds
Granulated sugar

**1.** Beat butter at medium speed with an electric mixer until creamy; gradually add brown sugar, beating well. Add egg, anise extract, and almond extract, beating well.

**2.** Combine flour and next 8 ingredients; stir well. Gradually add to butter mixture, beating at low speed until blended. Stir in chopped almonds.

**3.** Divide dough in half. Shape 1 portion into a ball; knead 3 or 4 times until smooth. Roll dough into a 9-inch square on a lightly greased baking sheet. Cut dough into 36 (1½-inch) squares. Press a whole almond into center of each square. Repeat procedure with remaining dough.

**4.** Bake at 325° for 25 minutes. Cool slightly on baking sheet, and sprinkle with sugar while warm; remove to wire racks to cool completely. Break cookies apart, and store in airtight containers.

# sparkling ginger stars

A heavy sugar crust and the peppery bite of fresh ginger make these gingerbread cookies anything but ordinary. Be sure your spices are fresh; that will make a big taste difference here.

prep: 12 min.   cook: 17 min. per batch   other: 2 hr., 30 min.   makes 2 dozen

1½  cups all-purpose flour
½   tsp. baking soda
½   tsp. salt
2   tsp. ground ginger
1   tsp. ground cinnamon
¼   tsp. ground cloves
¼   tsp. freshly grated nutmeg
½   cup unsalted butter, softened
½   cup firmly packed dark brown sugar
¼   cup dark molasses
1   egg yolk
1   Tbsp. grated lemon rind
1   Tbsp. grated fresh ginger
½   tsp. vanilla extract
1   large egg
2   Tbsp. whipping cream
1   (3.25-oz.) jar coarse sparkling sugar (see note)

**1.** Combine first 7 ingredients in a medium bowl; stir until blended.

**2.** Beat butter at medium speed with an electric mixer until creamy; gradually add dark brown sugar, beating well. Add molasses and next 4 ingredients, beating well. Gradually add flour mixture, beating just until blended.

**3.** Shape dough into a ball, and divide in half. Flatten each half into a round disk; wrap each in plastic wrap, and chill 2½ hours until firm.

**4.** Roll out dough, 1 portion at a time, to ¼-inch thickness on a lightly floured surface. Cut into star shapes, using a 4-inch cookie cutter. Place ½ inch apart on parchment paper-lined baking sheets.

**5.** Whisk together 1 egg and whipping cream; brush egg wash lightly over cookies. Sprinkle heavily with sparkling sugar.

**6.** Bake at 325° for 17 minutes or until cookies are puffed and slightly darker around edges. Cool 2 minutes on baking sheets; remove with parchment paper to wire racks to cool completely.

**Note:** Sparkling sugar can be purchased at gourmet grocery stores or cake decorating shops, or ordered from La Cuisine at 800-521-1176 or lacuisineus.com.

# classic sugar cookies

Cut this dough into a variety of your favorite shapes. The dippable glaze will transform the cookies into works of art almost too pretty to eat.

prep: 25 min.    cook: 10 min. per batch    other: 1 hr.    **makes 20 cookies**

1    cup butter or margarine, softened
1    cup granulated sugar
1    large egg
1    tsp. vanilla extract
3    cups all-purpose flour
¼    tsp. salt
Glaze
1    (3.25-oz.) jar coarse sparkling sugar

**1.** Beat butter at medium speed with an electric mixer until creamy. Gradually add granulated sugar, beating well. Add egg and vanilla, beating well. Combine flour and salt. Gradually add to butter mixture, beating until blended. Divide dough in half. Cover; chill 1 hour.

**2.** Roll each portion of dough to ¼-inch thickness on a lightly floured surface. Cut with desired cookie cutters. (We used flower and starfish cutters.) Place on lightly greased baking sheets.

**3.** Bake at 350° for 8 to 10 minutes or until edges of cookies are lightly browned. Cool cookies 1 minute on baking sheets, and remove to wire racks to cool completely.

**4.** Dip cookies in Glaze and sprinkle, while wet, with sparkling sugar.

## glaze

prep: 5 min.    makes 1⅓ cups

1    (16-oz.) package powdered sugar
6    Tbsp. warm water
Liquid food coloring (optional)

**1.** Stir together powdered sugar and warm water using a wire whisk. Divide mixture, and tint with food coloring, if desired; place in shallow bowls for ease in dipping cookies.

# chocolate-orange swirls

Freshly grated rind accentuates the orange flavor in these memorable cookies.

prep: 25 min.   cook: 12 min. per batch   other: 2 hr.   makes 2½ dozen

1    cup butter, softened
1    cup sugar
1    large egg
1    tsp. vanilla extract
3    cups all-purpose flour
1½  tsp. baking powder
¼    tsp. salt
1    tsp. grated orange rind
1½  tsp. orange extract
2    (1-oz.) semisweet chocolate baking squares,
      melted and cooled

**1.** Beat butter at medium speed with an electric mixer until creamy; gradually add sugar, beating well. Add egg and vanilla; beat well.

**2.** Combine flour, baking powder, and salt. Gradually add flour mixture to butter mixture, beating at low speed until blended.

**3.** Remove half of dough from bowl. Add orange rind and orange extract to dough in bowl, and beat well. Remove orange dough from mixing bowl, and set aside. Return plain dough to mixing bowl; add melted chocolate, beating well. Cover and chill both portions of dough 1 hour.

**4.** Roll each half of dough to a 15- x 8-inch rectangle on floured wax paper. Place orange dough on top of chocolate dough; peel off top wax paper. Tightly roll dough, jelly-roll fashion, starting at short side and peeling wax paper from dough while rolling. Cover and chill 1 hour.

**5.** Slice dough into ¼-inch-thick slices; place on ungreased baking sheets.

**6.** Bake at 350° for 10 to 12 minutes. Remove to wire racks to cool.

**Note:** To prevent flat-sided cookies, turn dough roll halfway through the second chilling time. Dental floss makes cutting the dough easier.

*Remember me rosemary* Fresh rosemary adds a fragrant quality to these delicate cookies. And because the herb traditionally represents remembrance, a batch of these treats is ideal as a thank-you or birthday gift. Serve them with a hot cup of your favorite tea or atop a cool scoop of sherbet.

## rosemary shortbread cookies

prep: 15 min.   cook: 20 min. per batch   makes 1½ dozen

1½  cups all-purpose flour
½   cup butter, chilled
¼   cup sifted powdered sugar
2   Tbsp. minced fresh rosemary
2   Tbsp. granulated sugar

**1.** Process first 4 ingredients in a food processor until mixture forms a ball.
**2.** Roll dough to ¼-inch thickness on a lightly floured surface. Cut with a 2-inch cookie cutter; place on lightly greased baking sheets.
**3.** Bake at 325° for 18 to 20 minutes or until edges are lightly browned. Sprinkle with granulated sugar. Remove to wire racks to cool completely.

# chewy coffee-toffee shortbread

Toffee bits give this golden shortbread its slightly chewy texture.

prep: 20 min.   cook: 50 min. per batch   other: 30 min.   makes 16 cookies

1    cup butter, softened
½    cup firmly packed light brown sugar
1    Tbsp. instant espresso powder (we tested with Café Bustelo)
1    Tbsp. hot water
2¼   cups all-purpose flour
⅛    tsp. salt
½    cup toffee bits (we tested with Hershey's Heath Bits O' Brickle Toffee Bits)

**1.** Beat butter at medium speed with an electric mixer until creamy; gradually add sugar, beating well. Stir together espresso powder and water. Add to butter mixture, stirring well.

**2.** Combine flour and salt; gradually add to butter mixture, beating at low speed until blended. Stir in toffee bits. Cover and chill dough 30 minutes.

**3.** Roll dough to ½-inch thickness on a lightly floured surface. Cut with a 2½-inch round cutter. Place 2 inches apart on ungreased baking sheets.

**4.** Bake at 275° for 50 minutes. Cool 2 minutes on baking sheets. Remove to wire racks to cool completely.

**Note:** If you can't find toffee bits in the supermarket, substitute ½ cup finely crushed Skor candy bars or crushed Werther's Original candies.

*Tea time* Tea cakes have a connection to Girl Scouts of the USA. "In 1912, Juliette Gordon Low held many organizational teas when she was starting the Girl Scouts, where she was known for serving her 'little cakes'," says Katherine Keena, program manager at the Juliette Gordon Low birthplace in Savannah, Georgia.

## tea cakes

prep: 20 min.   cook: 12 min. per batch   other: 1 hr.   **makes 3 dozen**

1    cup butter, softened
2    cups sugar
3    large eggs
1    tsp. vanilla extract
3½  cups all-purpose flour
1    tsp. baking soda
½   tsp. salt

**1.** Beat butter at medium speed with an electric mixer until creamy; gradually add sugar, beating well. Add eggs, 1 at a time, beating until blended after each addition. Add vanilla, beating until blended.

**2.** Combine flour, baking soda, and salt; gradually add to butter mixture, beating at low speed until blended.

**3.** Divide dough in half; wrap each portion in plastic wrap, and chill 1 hour. Roll half of dough to ¼-inch thickness on a lightly floured surface. Cut with a 2½-inch round cutter, and place 1 inch apart on parchment paper-lined baking sheets.

**4.** Bake at 350° for 10 to 12 minutes or until edges begin to brown; cool on baking sheets 5 minutes. Remove to wire racks to cool completely. Repeat procedure with remaining dough.

# jam kolache

Four-ingredient gems with a flavorful burst of strawberry jam tucked inside, these little treats are the big attraction at the annual Kolache Festival. This Caldwell, Texas, event is more than 20 years old and is hosted by proud descendants of early Czechoslovakian immigrants to Central Texas.

**prep: 16 min.   cook: 15 min. per batch   makes 3½ dozen**

½   cup butter or margarine, softened
1   (3-oz.) package cream cheese, softened
1¼  cups all-purpose flour
Strawberry jam (about ½ cup)

**1.** Beat butter and cream cheese at medium speed with an electric mixer until creamy. Add flour to butter mixture, beating well.
**2.** Roll dough to ⅛-inch thickness on a lightly floured surface; cut with a 2½-inch round cookie cutter. Place on lightly greased baking sheets. Spoon ¼ tsp. jam on each cookie. Fold opposite sides to center, slightly overlapping edges; press down lightly on centers.
**3.** Bake at 375° for 15 minutes. Remove to wire racks to cool.

# date pinwheel cookies

Slather this dough with date-nut filling, roll it jelly-roll fashion, and then slice and bake it into pretty cookies. We found it easier to slice these cookies with an electric knife.

prep: 20 min.   cook: 14 min. per batch   other: 2 hr.   makes 4 dozen

1   (10-oz.) package chopped dates
¾   cup granulated sugar, divided
¼   tsp. salt, divided
1   cup chopped walnuts
½   cup butter or margarine, softened
½   cup firmly packed brown sugar
1   large egg
½   tsp. vanilla extract
2   cups all-purpose flour
¼   tsp. baking soda

**1.** Stir together dates, ¼ cup granulated sugar, ½ cup water, and ⅛ tsp. salt in a saucepan; bring mixture to a boil over medium-high heat. Reduce heat; simmer 3 to 5 minutes. Remove from heat; stir in walnuts, and set aside.

**2.** Beat remaining ½ cup granulated sugar, softened butter, and brown sugar at medium speed with an electric mixer until light and fluffy.

**3.** Add egg and vanilla, beating until blended. Combine remaining ⅛ tsp. salt, flour, and baking soda. Gradually add to butter mixture, beating until blended after each addition. Cover and chill 1 hour.

**4.** Turn dough out onto lightly floured wax paper, and roll into an 18- x 12-inch rectangle. Spread date mixture over dough, leaving a ½-inch border.

**5.** Roll up dough, jelly-roll fashion, beginning at 1 long side. Wrap in wax paper, and chill 1 hour.

**6.** Cut roll into ¼-inch-thick slices; place on lightly greased baking sheets.

**7.** Bake at 375° for 12 to 14 minutes or until lightly browned. Cool 2 to 3 minutes on baking sheets, and remove to wire racks to cool completely.

# linzer cookies

A twist on Austria's linzer torte—a tart with a nutty crust, preserve filling, and lattice top—these cookies have a fitting Southern lineage. The dough boasts toasted chopped pecans. The top pecan producer in this country, at approximately 100 million pounds per year, is Georgia, home to the earliest documented Austrian settlers in America. They arrived in the colony in 1734. One of these settlers, Johann Adam Treutlen, even became the first elected governor of the new state.

prep: 25 min.   cook: 15 min. per batch   other: 1 hr.   makes 3 dozen

1¼ cups butter, softened
1   cup powdered sugar, sifted
2½ cups all-purpose flour
½   cup finely chopped pecans, toasted
1   tsp. grated lemon rind
¼   tsp. salt
¼   tsp. ground cloves
¼   tsp. ground cinnamon
¼   cup seedless raspberry jam
Powdered sugar

**1.** Beat butter at medium speed with an electric mixer until creamy; gradually add 1 cup powdered sugar, beating until light and fluffy.

**2.** Combine flour and next 5 ingredients; gradually add to butter mixture, beating just until blended.

**3.** Divide dough into 2 portions. Cover; chill 1 hour.

**4.** Roll each portion to ⅛-inch thickness on a lightly floured surface. Cut with a 3-inch star-shaped cutter; cut centers out of half of cookies with 1½-inch star-shaped cutter. Or use a 2-inch round cutter, and cut centers out of half with 1-inch round cutter. Place all cookies on lightly greased baking sheets.

**5.** Bake at 325° for 15 minutes; remove to wire racks to cool completely.

**6.** Spread all large solid cookies and half of small cookies with jam; sprinkle remaining cookies with powdered sugar. Top each large solid cookie with a hollow cookie and each small cookie with jam with a small plain cookie.

# cream cheese crescents

A version of the European Jewish pastry rugelach, these cookies are another testament to the Southern foodways' varied influences.

prep: 45 min.   cook: 20 min. per batch   other: 8 hr., 30 min.   makes 32 cookies

1   cup butter, softened
1   (8-oz.) package cream cheese, softened
½   cup sugar
2¾   cups all-purpose flour
½   tsp. salt
Cranberry-Pecan Filling
1   large egg, lightly beaten
½   cup granulated sugar or sparkling sugar

**1.** Beat butter and cream cheese at medium speed with an electric mixer until creamy; gradually add ½ cup sugar, beating until fluffy. Combine flour and salt. Stir into butter mixture until blended.
**2.** Divide dough into 4 equal portions; flatten each portion into a disk, and wrap each disk separately in plastic wrap. Chill 8 hours.

**3.** Roll 1 portion of dough at a time into an 8-inch circle on a lightly floured surface (keep remaining dough chilled until ready to use). Spread with 3 heaping tablespoonfuls Cranberry-Pecan Filling, leaving a ½-inch border around edge. Using a sharp knife, cut circle into 8 wedges; roll up each wedge, starting at wide end, to form a crescent shape. Place crescents, point side down, on parchment paper-lined baking sheets. Chill cookies on baking sheets 30 minutes.
**4.** Combine egg and 2 Tbsp. water in a small bowl; brush cookies gently with egg wash, and sprinkle with ½ cup sugar.
**5.** Bake at 350° for 18 to 20 minutes or until golden. Remove to wire racks to cool completely.

# cranberry-pecan filling

prep: 10 min.   makes about 1 cup

⅔   cup sugar
½   cup finely chopped pecans, toasted
½   cup finely chopped sweetened dried cranberries*
¼   cup butter, melted
1½   tsp. ground cinnamon
¾   tsp. ground allspice

**1.** Stir together all ingredients until blended.

*Substitute ⅔ cup finely chopped dried cherries or apricots, if desired.

**Mudslide Brownies,** page 96

# bar
# cookies

Can't decide between cookies or cake? Bar none…these pan-baked cookies are especially versatile. They're that "in between" dessert that fits any occasion—from after the ballgame to casual get-togethers. Cut big squares of cakelike bar cookies after even the most elegant dinner and top each with a scoop of ice cream and a strawberry. Save those with dense fillings for care packages or after-school snacks.

## These secrets will lead to great bar cookies:

• For everyday bar cookies, simply cut slices out of the pan as you want them. When you want to cut and serve extra-neat slices, use the foil-lining trick. Just line a lightly greased pan with foil and spray the foil with vegetable cooking spray before spreading the batter into it to bake. After baking, use foil to lift un-cut cookies out of pan. Peel foil away, and cut cookies into squares.

• If you like soft, chewy bar cookies, remove them from the oven at the lower end of the bake time. For firmer cookies, bake for the longer time suggested.

• Make sure the cookies are completely cooled in the pan before cutting them into portions. You can freeze them for several minutes to make cutting them easier.

• When cutting brownies, use a plastic knife for smoother edges. You'll never want to cut brownies with a regular knife again once you see the clean slices this humble plastic utensil makes.

• Remember that bake times will change if you use a pan of a different size or made of a different material. Expect thinner brownies and shorter baking time in larger pans.

# cheesecake swirl squares

Cheesecake brownies get a splash of rum flavor and extra richness from eggnog. Cut them into large bars for a special-occasion splurge.

**prep: 26 min.    cook: 41 min.    other: 1 hr.**    makes 1 dozen

| | |
|---|---|
| 55 | vanilla wafers, crushed |
| 6 | Tbsp. butter or margarine, melted |
| ½ | cup finely chopped pecans, toasted |
| 2 | (8-oz.) packages cream cheese, softened |
| ½ | cup sugar |
| 1½ | tsp. rum extract |
| 2 | large eggs |
| ¼ | cup refrigerated eggnog |
| ½ | cup white chocolate morsels, melted |
| ½ | cup double chocolate morsels, melted (we tested with Ghirardelli), or regular semisweet morsels |

**1.** Combine first 3 ingredients in a large bowl, stirring until blended. Press crumb mixture into bottom of a lightly greased 8-inch or 9-inch square pan. Bake at 350° for 8 minutes and cool.

**2.** Beat softened cream cheese, sugar, and rum extract at medium speed with an electric mixer just until smooth. Add eggs, 1 at a time, beating just until blended after each addition. Pour 1½ cups cream cheese batter over baked crust.

**3.** Stir eggnog into remaining batter. Divide mixture in half; stir melted white chocolate into 1 portion, and spoon over cream cheese mixture. Stir melted semi-sweet chocolate into remaining batter. Drop spoonfuls of chocolate batter over white chocolate layer; gently swirl batters with a knife.

**4.** Bake at 350° for 30 to 33 minutes or until almost set. Cool in pan on a wire rack. Cover and chill at least 1 hour before serving. Cut into squares.

# chocolate chip cheesecake bars

Take these festive bars to your next gathering—you can make them ahead of time and transport them easily.

prep: 15 min.    cook: 40 min.    other: 4 hr.    makes 1 dozen

| | |
|---|---|
| 1 | cup all-purpose flour |
| ⅓ | cup firmly packed light brown sugar |
| ¼ | cup butter, softened |
| 3 | (8-oz.) packages cream cheese, softened |
| ¾ | cup granulated sugar |
| 3 | large eggs |
| ⅓ | cup sour cream |
| ½ | tsp. vanilla extract |
| 1 | (12-oz.) package semisweet chocolate mini morsels, divided (we tested with Nestlé Toll House) |

**1.** Beat first 3 ingredients at medium-low speed with an electric mixer until combined. Increase speed to medium, and beat until well blended and crumbly. Pat mixture into a lightly greased 13- x 9-inch pan.

**2.** Bake at 350° for 13 to 15 minutes or until lightly browned.

**3.** Beat cream cheese at medium speed with electric mixer until creamy. Gradually add granulated sugar, beating until well blended. Add eggs, 1 at a time, beating at low speed just until blended after each addition. Add sour cream, vanilla, and 1 cup chocolate morsels, beating just until blended. Pour over baked crust.

**4.** Bake at 350° for 25 minutes or until set. Cool in pan on a wire rack.

**5.** Microwave remaining chocolate morsels in a 2-cup glass measuring cup on HIGH 1 minute, stirring after 30 seconds. Stir until smooth. Transfer to a 1-qt. zip-top plastic freezer bag; cut a tiny hole in 1 corner of bag. Pipe melted chocolate over cheesecake by gently squeezing bag. Cover and chill at least 4 hours; cut into bars.

*Tropical treat* For a cooling, summer dessert, you won't go wrong with this bar cookie variation of the classic Key lime pie. Found in the southernmost tip of Florida, Key limes are small, yellow, and have a tarter flavor than other lime varieties. Macadamias contribute to the perfect crust for this creamy filling.

# key lime squares with macadamia crust

prep: 25 min.   cook: 20 min.   other: 8 hr.   **makes 2 dozen**

2     cups all-purpose flour
½     cup firmly packed light brown sugar
⅔     cup chopped macadamias
6     Tbsp. butter, cubed
½     tsp. salt
¾     cup granulated sugar
½     cup Key lime juice
1     envelope unflavored gelatin
2     Tbsp. Key lime juice
1     (14-oz.) can sweetened condensed milk
1     tsp. grated lime rind
2½   cups whipping cream, whipped
Garnish: grated Key lime rind

**1.** Process first 5 ingredients in a food processor until finely ground. Press mixture into a greased aluminum foil-lined 13- x 9-inch pan, allowing foil to extend over edges of pan.

**2.** Bake at 350° for 20 minutes or until golden. Cool on a wire rack.

**3.** Heat granulated sugar and ½ cup Key lime juice over low heat, stirring until sugar dissolves. Remove from heat, and set aside.

**4.** Sprinkle gelatin over 2 Tbsp. Key lime juice in a medium bowl; stir gelatin mixture, and let stand 3 to 5 minutes.

**5.** Add hot mixture to gelatin mixture, stirring until gelatin dissolves. Whisk in sweetened condensed milk and 1 tsp. grated lime rind.

**6.** Place bowl in a larger bowl filled with ice; whisk mixture 10 minutes or until partially set.

**7.** Fold in whipped cream. Pour over prepared crust; cover and chill 8 hours. Use foil to lift out of pan. Peel foil away, and cut into squares. Garnish, if desired.

*"Mint" to be delicious* A dash of mint extract gives these buttery shortbread cookies an extra splash of flavor. Choose peppermint or spearmint extract to give them the flavor twist you prefer; then serve them with hot mint tea or a tall glass of sweet tea and a slice of fresh lemon. For ease, you won't beat this recipe. The dough is pressed onto a jelly-roll pan, baked, and then cut into squares. For showers or tea parties, cut them into diamond shapes.

## butter-mint shortbread

prep: 10 min.   cook: 20 min.   makes 3 dozen

1    cup butter, softened
¾   cup powdered sugar
½   tsp. mint extract
½   tsp. vanilla extract
2¼  cups all-purpose flour
Powdered sugar

**1.** Beat butter and ¾ cup powdered sugar at medium speed with an electric mixer until creamy. Add extracts, beating until blended. Gradually add flour, beating at low speed until blended. Press dough into an ungreased 15- x 10-inch jelly-roll pan.

**2.** Bake at 325° for 20 minutes or until golden. Cool in pan on a wire rack 10 minutes. Cut into squares; sprinkle with powdered sugar. Remove to wire racks to cool completely.

# chunky chocolate brownies

Chocolate chunks make these brownies fudgy; use the 23-minute baking time to make them extra gooey.

**prep: 20 min.   cook: 28 min.   other: 5 min.**   makes 9 brownies

¾   cup granulated sugar
⅓   cup butter
1   (11.5-oz.) package semisweet chocolate chunks, divided
2   large eggs
1   tsp. vanilla extract
½   cup chopped hazelnuts or pecans, toasted
¾   cup all-purpose flour
¼   tsp. salt
Powdered sugar

**1.** Combine 2 Tbsp. water, granulated sugar, and butter in a 3½-qt. saucepan. Bring to a boil over medium heat, stirring constantly. Remove from heat, and stir in 1 cup chocolate chunks until smooth. Let cool 5 minutes.

**2.** Add eggs, 1 at a time, stirring just until blended. Stir in vanilla.

**3.** Stir in remaining chocolate chunks and hazelnuts. Combine flour and salt; stir flour mixture into chocolate mixture. Spread into a lightly greased 9-inch square pan.

**4.** Bake at 325° for 23 to 28 minutes. Cool in pan on a wire rack. Dust with powdered sugar. Cut into squares.

**To freeze up to 3 months:** Wrap baked brownies in aluminum foil, and place in a large zip-top plastic freezer bag. To thaw, remove brownies from plastic bag, and let stand at room temperature for 3 hours; unwrap and serve.

# Bayou brownies

Don't think chocolate when you try these brownies. Instead, think pecans and a sweet cream cheese topping. Yellow cake mix makes the recipe extra convenient for busy cooks to whip up in minutes.

**prep: 10 min.    cook: 40 min.    makes 15 brownies**

1    cup chopped pecans
½    cup butter, melted
3    large eggs, divided
1    (18.25-oz.) package yellow cake mix
1    (8-oz.) package cream cheese, softened
1    (16-oz.) package powdered sugar

**1.** Combine pecans, butter, 1 egg, and cake mix, stirring until well blended; press in bottom of a lightly greased 13- x 9-inch pan.
**2.** Beat remaining 2 eggs, cream cheese, and powdered sugar at medium speed with an electric mixer until smooth. Pour over cake mix layer.
**3.** Bake at 325° for 40 minutes or until set. Cool in pan on a wire rack. Cut into squares.

# gingerbread squares with lemon-cream cheese frosting

prep: 20 min.　cook: 25 min.　makes 2 to 3 dozen

1¾ cups all-purpose flour

2　tsp. ground cinnamon

2　tsp. ground ginger

½　tsp. baking soda

¼　tsp. salt

1　cup butter, softened

½　cup granulated sugar

½　cup firmly packed light brown sugar

1　large egg

⅓　cup molasses

3　Tbsp. milk

Lemon-Cream Cheese Frosting

Garnish: grated lemon rind

**1.** Combine first 5 ingredients. Set aside.

**2.** Beat butter at medium speed with an electric mixer until creamy. Gradually add sugars, beating until well blended. Add egg, beating until blended. Reduce speed to low; gradually add flour mixture, beating just until blended. Add molasses and milk, beating just until blended. Spread batter in a lightly greased 13- x 9-inch pan.

**3.** Bake at 350° for 25 minutes or until a wooden pick inserted in center comes out clean. Cool in pan on a wire rack. Spread with Lemon-Cream Cheese Frosting. Cut into squares. Garnish with grated lemon rind, if desired. Cut each bar in half, forming 2 triangles if desired.

**Note:** Frosted bars may be stored in an airtight container in the refrigerator 5 to 7 days. If you decide to freeze these bars, do not frost them before freezing. Add the frosting to partially thawed bars, and then cut into shapes.

## lemon-cream cheese frosting

prep: 10 min.　makes about 2 cups

2　(3-oz.) packages cream cheese, softened

2　Tbsp. butter, softened

¼　cup lemon curd

1　tsp. grated lemon rind

2½ cups powdered sugar

**1.** Beat cream cheese and butter at medium speed with an electric mixer until creamy. Add lemon curd and lemon rind, beating until blended. Gradually add powdered sugar, beating until smooth.

# double chocolate brownies with caramel frosting

prep: 15 min.   cook: 40 min.   **makes 32 brownies**

2   (1-oz.) unsweetened chocolate baking squares
2   (1-oz.) semisweet chocolate baking squares
1   cup butter, softened
2   cups sugar
4   large eggs
1   cup all-purpose flour
½   tsp. salt
1   tsp. vanilla extract
¾   cup chopped pecans, toasted and divided
¾   cup semisweet chocolate morsels, divided
Caramel Frosting

**1.** Microwave chocolate squares in a small microwave-safe bowl at MEDIUM (50% power) 1½ minutes or until melted. Stir chocolate until smooth.
**2.** Beat butter and sugar at medium speed with an electric mixer until creamy. Add eggs, 1 at a time, beating just until blended after each addition. Add melted chocolate, beating just until blended.
**3.** Add flour and salt, beating at low speed just until blended. Stir in vanilla, ½ cup pecans, and ½ cup chocolate morsels. Spread batter into a greased and floured 13- x 9-inch pan. Sprinkle with remaining ¼ cup pecans and ¼ cup chocolate morsels.
**4.** Bake at 350° for 40 minutes or until set. Cool in pan on a wire rack. Spread with Caramel Frosting. Cut into squares.

## caramel frosting

prep: 10 min.   cook: 30 min.   makes 2 cups

¾   cup butter
2   cups sugar
½   cup buttermilk
12   large marshmallows
1   Tbsp. light corn syrup
½   tsp. baking soda

**1.** Melt butter in a large saucepan over low heat. Stir in remaining ingredients. Cook over medium heat, stirring occasionally, 25 to 30 minutes or until a candy thermometer registers 234° (soft ball stage).
**2.** Remove from heat. Beat at high speed 5 to 7 minutes or until frosting thickens and begins to lose its gloss.

# death-by-caramel squares

These showy brownies are nice and tall, with pockets of soft caramel. They are wicked enough on their own; but for an over-the-top dessert, add a scoop of vanilla ice cream and a drizzle of caramel sauce.

prep: 24 min.   cook: 1 hr., 5 min.   makes 2 dozen

3   cups firmly packed light brown sugar
2   cups unsalted butter, melted
3   large eggs, lightly beaten
1   Tbsp. vanilla extract
4   cups all-purpose flour
1   cup uncooked regular oats
1   tsp. baking powder
½   tsp. baking soda
¾   tsp. salt
6   (2.07-oz.) chocolate-coated caramel-peanut nougat bars, chopped (we tested with Snickers)
1   (14-oz.) can dulce de leche (see note)

**1.** Combine first 4 ingredients in a large bowl; stir well. Combine flour and next 4 ingredients. Add to butter mixture, stirring just until blended. Fold in chopped candy bars.

**2.** Spoon batter into a greased aluminum foil-lined 13- x 9-inch pan coated with cooking spray, allowing foil to extend over edges of pan. (Pan will be very full.) Spoon dollops of dulce de leche over batter; swirl slightly into batter with a knife.

**3.** Bake at 325° for 1 hour and 5 minutes. Cool in a pan on a wire rack. (This may take several hours.) Use foil to lift uncut brownies out of pan. Peel foil away, and cut into squares.

**Note:** Find dulce de leche with other ethnic ingredients or on the baking aisle.

# mudslide brownies

Yummy ingredients from the popular drink make a splash in these decadent bars.

prep: 21 min.   cook: 25 min.   makes 3 dozen small or 1 dozen large

6    (1-oz.) unsweetened chocolate baking squares, divided
½    cup plus 2 Tbsp. unsalted butter, divided
1    cup granulated sugar
1    cup firmly packed light brown sugar
3    large eggs
4    tsp. instant espresso powder, divided (we tested with Café Bustelo)
2    Tbsp. plus 2 tsp. coffee liqueur, divided
1½  cups all-purpose flour
½    tsp. salt
1    cup chopped pecans, toasted
2    Tbsp. whipping cream or half-and-half
2    Tbsp. vodka
2¼ to 2½ cups powdered sugar
Garnish: chocolate-covered espresso coffee beans, chopped

**1.** Melt 4 chocolate baking squares and ½ cup butter in a heavy saucepan over low heat, stirring occasionally. Remove from heat, and transfer to a large bowl. Add sugars; stir well. Stir in eggs, 2 tsp. espresso powder, and 2 tsp. coffee liqueur. Add flour and salt, stirring until blended. Stir in pecans.

**2.** Spread batter into a lightly greased aluminum foil-lined 13- x 9-inch pan (or see note).

**3.** Bake at 325° for 20 to 25 minutes or until brownies appear set on top. Cool in pan on a wire rack.

**4.** Melt remaining 2 chocolate baking squares and 2 Tbsp. butter in heavy saucepan over low heat, stirring occasionally. Remove from heat; transfer to a medium bowl. Stir in remaining 2 tsp. espresso powder, 2 Tbsp. coffee liqueur, whipping cream, and vodka. Add enough powdered sugar for good spreading consistency, beating at medium speed with an electric mixer until smooth.

**5.** Spread frosting over cooled brownies; garnish, if desired. Let stand until frosting is set. Use foil to lift uncut brownies out of pan. Peel foil away, and cut into squares.

**Note:** For really thick, showy brownies, we baked these in an 11- x 7-inch pan at 325° for 26 to 28 minutes.

# peanut butter-candy bar brownies

Peanut butter sandwich cookies become the crumb crust for these hunky bars loaded with chunks of your favorite candy bars.

prep: 26 min.   cook: 35 min.   makes 28 small bars or 18 large bars

1   (16-oz.) package peanut-shaped peanut butter sandwich cookies, crushed
½   cup butter, melted
1   (14-oz.) can sweetened condensed milk
½   cup creamy peanut butter
1   Tbsp. vanilla extract
5   (1.5-oz.) packages chocolate-covered peanut butter cup candies, coarsely chopped
2   (2.1-oz.) chocolate-covered crispy peanut buttery candy bars, coarsely chopped (we tested with Butterfinger)
1   cup semisweet chocolate morsels
½   cup honey-roasted peanuts
½   cup sweetened flaked coconut

**1.** Combine crushed cookies and butter in a medium bowl. Press crumb mixture into bottom of a greased aluminum foil-lined 13- x 9-inch pan, allowing foil to extend over edges of pan. Bake at 350° for 6 to 8 minutes.

**2.** Combine condensed milk, peanut butter, and vanilla in a medium bowl, stirring until smooth.

**3.** Sprinkle chopped candy bars, chocolate morsels, peanuts, and coconut over crust. Drizzle condensed milk mixture over coconut.

**4.** Bake at 350° for 27 minutes or until lightly browned. Cool in pan on a wire rack. Use foil to lift uncut brownies out of pan. Peel foil away, and cut into squares.

# cappuccino-frosted brownies

These delicious little treats received our Test Kitchens' highest rating.

prep: 20 min.   cook: 35 min.   **makes 1 dozen**

4   (1-oz.) unsweetened chocolate baking squares,
    coarsely chopped
¾   cup butter
2   cups sugar
4   large eggs
1   cup all-purpose flour
1   tsp. vanilla extract
1   cup semisweet chocolate morsels
Cappuccino Buttercream Frosting
Garnish: chopped chocolate-covered
    espresso coffee beans

**1.** Microwave chopped chocolate and butter in a large microwave-safe bowl at HIGH 1½ minutes, stirring after 1 minute and at end or until melted and smooth. Stir in sugar. Add eggs, 1 at a time, beating with a spoon just until blended after each addition.
**2.** Stir in flour and vanilla; stir in chocolate morsels. Pour mixture into a lightly greased 13- x 9-inch pan.
**3.** Bake at 350° for 30 to 35 minutes or until a wooden pick inserted in center comes out clean. Cool in pan on a wire rack.
**4.** Spread Cappuccino Buttercream Frosting over top of cooled brownies. Cut into squares, and garnish, if desired. Cover and chill, if desired.

## cappuccino buttercream frosting

prep: 10 min.   other: 10 min.   makes 1½ cups

1   (1.16-oz.) envelope instant mocha cappuccino mix
    (we tested with Land O' Lakes Suisse Mocha Hot
    Cappuccino Mix)
¼   cup hot milk
½   cup butter, softened
1   (16-oz.) package powdered sugar

**1.** Dissolve instant mocha cappuccino mix in hot milk in a small cup, stirring to combine; cool completely. Pour milk mixture into a mixing bowl; add softened butter, and beat at medium speed with an electric mixer until well combined.
**2.** Gradually add powdered sugar, beating until smooth and fluffy.

*This pie is square* Pecan pie in cookie-size squares—that's what you'll get when you make this recipe. As a classic Southern dessert synonymous with Georgia, Louisiana, and Texas, pecan pie makes an appearance in most Southern cookbooks. The original version came about when Karo corn syrup was introduced in the early 1900s, and several states lay claim to this version. In this bar cookie version, honey replaces the syrup for the gooey filling cradled in a shortbread-style crust.

## pecan pie squares

Use salted butter and bring the filling to a rolling boil before pouring it over the crust.

**prep: 20 min.   cook: 50 min.   makes about 28 squares**

| | |
|---|---|
| 2 | cups all-purpose flour |
| ⅔ | cup powdered sugar |
| ¾ | cup butter, softened |
| ½ | cup firmly packed brown sugar |
| ½ | cup honey |
| ⅔ | cup butter |
| 3 | Tbsp. whipping cream |
| 3½ | cups coarsely chopped pecans |

**1.** Sift together flour and powdered sugar. Cut in ¾ cup softened butter using a pastry blender or fork just until mixture resembles coarse meal. Pat mixture on bottom and 1½ inches up sides of a lightly greased 13- x 9-inch baking dish.

**2.** Bake at 350° for 20 minutes or until edges are lightly browned. Cool. Bring brown sugar, honey, ⅔ cup butter, and whipping cream to a boil in a saucepan over medium-high heat. Stir in pecans, and pour hot filling into prepared crust.

**3.** Bake at 350° for 25 to 30 minutes or until golden and bubbly. Cool in pan on a wire rack before cutting into 2-inch squares.

# oatmeal carmelitas

Caramels, chocolate morsels, and pecans combine for a melt-in-your-mouth treat.

prep: 25 min.   cook: 30 min.   makes 24 to 30 carmelitas

2   cups all-purpose flour
2   cups uncooked quick-cooking oats
1½  cups firmly packed light brown sugar
1   tsp. baking soda
¼   tsp. salt
1   cup butter, melted
1   (12-oz.) package semisweet chocolate morsels
½   cup chopped pecans or walnuts, toasted (optional)
1   (14-oz.) package caramels
⅓   cup half-and-half

**1.** Stir together first 5 ingredients in a large mixing bowl. Add butter, stirring until mixture is crumbly. Reserve half of mixture (about 2¾ cups). Press remaining half of mixture into bottom of a greased aluminum foil-lined 13- x 9-inch pan, allowing foil to extend over edges of pan. Sprinkle with chocolate morsels and, if desired, pecans.

**2.** Microwave caramels and ⅓ cup half-and-half in a microwave-safe bowl at MEDIUM (50% power) 3 minutes. Stir and microwave at MEDIUM 1 to 3 more minutes or until mixture is smooth. Let stand 1 minute. Pour over chocolate morsels. Sprinkle with reserved crumb mixture.

**3.** Bake at 350° for 30 minutes or until light golden brown. Cool in pan on a wire rack. Use foil to lift out of pan. Peel foil away, and cut into squares.

# kitchen sink brownies

Decadence abounds in each bite of these chunky, candy-studded brownies full of good things you probably have in the pantry.

prep: 22 min.　cook: 58 min.　other: 2 hr.　makes 2 dozen

1½　cups all-purpose flour

1　cup unsweetened cocoa

½　tsp. baking powder

¼　tsp. baking soda

¼　tsp. salt

1½　cups butter, melted

1½　cups granulated sugar

1½　cups firmly packed light brown sugar

4　large eggs

¼　cup brewed espresso or French roast coffee

2　tsp. vanilla extract

1　cup chopped cream-filled chocolate sandwich cookies (10 cookies)

4　(1.45-oz.) milk chocolate candy bars with almonds, chopped (we tested with Hershey's)

½　cup dark chocolate morsels (we tested with Ghirardelli)

½　cup white chocolate morsels

1　cup pecan pieces, toasted

**1.** Coat a 13- x 9-inch pan with cooking spray. Line pan with aluminum foil, allowing ends to hang over short sides of pan. Tuck overlapping ends under rim on short sides. Coat foil with cooking spray; set pan aside.

**2.** Combine flour and next 4 ingredients in a small bowl. Beat butter and sugars at medium speed with an electric mixer until smooth; add eggs, coffee, and vanilla, beating just until blended. Add flour mixture; beating at medium speed until blended. Stir in sandwich cookie crumbs and remaining 4 ingredients. Spoon batter into prepared pan, spreading evenly.

**3.** Bake at 325° for 55 to 58 minutes. Cool in pan on a wire rack. Cover and chill at least 2 hours.

**4.** Use foil to lift uncut brownies out of pan. Peel foil away, and cut into squares.

# metric equivalents

The recipes that appear in this cookbook use the standard U.S. method for measuring liquid and dry or solid ingredients (teaspoons, tablespoons, and cups). The information in the following charts is provided to help cooks outside the United States successfully use these recipes. All equivalents are approximate.

## Metric Equivalents for Different Types of Ingredients

A standard cup measure of a dry or solid ingredient will vary in weight depending on the type of ingredient. A standard cup of liquid is the same volume for any type of liquid. Use the following chart when converting standard cup measures to grams (weight) or to milliliters (volume).

| Standard Cup | Fine Powder (ex. flour) | Grain (ex. rice) | Granular (ex. sugar) | Liquid Solids (ex. butter) | Liquid (ex. milk) |
|---|---|---|---|---|---|
| 1 | 140 g | 150 g | 190 g | 200 g | 240 ml |
| ¾ | 105 g | 113 g | 143 g | 150 g | 180 ml |
| ⅔ | 93 g | 100 g | 125 g | 133 g | 160 ml |
| ½ | 70 g | 75 g | 95 g | 100 g | 120 ml |
| ⅓ | 47 g | 50 g | 63 g | 67 g | 80 ml |
| ¼ | 35 g | 38 g | 48 g | 50 g | 60 ml |
| ⅛ | 18 g | 19 g | 24 g | 25 g | 30 ml |

## Useful Equivalents for Dry Ingredients by Weight

(To convert ounces to grams, multiply the number of ounces by 30.)

| | | | | |
|---|---|---|---|---|
| 1 oz | = | ¹⁄₁₆ lb | = | 30 g |
| 4 oz | = | ¼ lb | = | 120 g |
| 8 oz | = | ½ lb | = | 240 g |
| 12 oz | = | ¾ lb | = | 360 g |
| 16 oz | = | 1 lb | = | 480 g |

## Useful Equivalents for Length

(To convert inches to centimeters, multiply the number of inches by 2.5.)

| | | | | | | |
|---|---|---|---|---|---|---|
| 1 in | | | | = | 2.5 cm | |
| 6 in | = | ½ ft | | = | 15 cm | |
| 12 in | = | 1 ft | | = | 30 cm | |
| 36 in | = | 3 ft | = 1 yd | = | 90 cm | |
| 40 in | | | | = | 100 cm | = 1 m |

## Useful Equivalents for Liquid Ingredients by Volume

| | | | | | | |
|---|---|---|---|---|---|---|
| ¼ tsp | | | | = | 1 ml | |
| ½ tsp | | | | = | 2 ml | |
| 1 tsp | | | | = | 5 ml | |
| 3 tsp | = | 1 Tbsp | = ½ fl oz | = | 15 ml | |
| | 2 Tbsp | = ⅛ cup | = 1 fl oz | = | 30 ml | |
| | 4 Tbsp | = ¼ cup | = 2 fl oz | = | 60 ml | |
| | 5⅓ Tbsp | = ⅓ cup | = 3 fl oz | = | 80 ml | |
| | 8 Tbsp | = ½ cup | = 4 fl oz | = | 120 ml | |
| | 10⅔ Tbsp | = ⅔ cup | = 5 fl oz | = | 160 ml | |
| | 12 Tbsp | = ¾ cup | = 6 fl oz | = | 180 ml | |
| | 16 Tbsp | = 1 cup | = 8 fl oz | = | 240 ml | |
| | 1 pt | = 2 cups | = 16 fl oz | = | 480 ml | |
| | 1 qt | = 4 cups | = 32 fl oz | = | 960 ml | |
| | | | 33 fl oz | = | 1000 ml | = 1 l |

## Useful Equivalents for Cooking/Oven Temperatures

| | Fahrenheit | Celsius | Gas Mark |
|---|---|---|---|
| Freeze water | 32° F | 0° C | |
| Room temperature | 68° F | 20° C | |
| Boil water | 212° F | 100° C | |
| Bake | 325° F | 160° C | 3 |
| | 350° F | 180° C | 4 |
| | 375° F | 190° C | 5 |
| | 400° F | 200° C | 6 |
| | 425° F | 220° C | 7 |
| | 450° F | 230° C | 8 |
| Broil | | | Grill |

# favorites

My family's favorite cookie recipes

| recipe | source/page | remarks |
| --- | --- | --- |
| | | |
| | | |
| | | |
| | | |
| | | |
| | | |
| | | |
| | | |
| | | |
| | | |
| | | |
| | | |

# index